This year marks the 14th year *The Independent* has presented Indies Arts Awards to individuals, groups and organizations who've made significant contributions to the local arts scene. This year's panel of judges was enthusiastic about our 2004 winners and their work in the community. "The Fruitful Five" include poet, educator, and organizer Dasan Ahanu, who spins poetry as effortlessly as he forges connections with Triangle's youth, voting activists and open mic crowds…

- Olufunke Moses, writer for the *Independent Weekly Magazine*

He travels a lot now, reading and teaching – which he sees as his obligation to the art. He has competed in slams nationally and he works with children, especially high-risk kids, and writes.

Ahanu is considered one of the top performance poets on the East Coast.

"It's important to get involved," he says, "I've been given the ability to put things down…I should use it."

- T.D. Mobley-Martinez, staff writer for *The State*

The Innovator
HPJ's Writeeasy Publishing
ISBN (Trade pbk.)
978-0-578-05108-6
Layout and Design: Chris Massenburg
Cover Art: Derrick "Benitez" Bryant
Inner Art: Ricardo "Tre" Dixon

HPJ's Writeeasy Publishing
Durham, North Carolina

www.dasanahanu.com

"The metaphor is perhaps one of man's most fruitful potentialities. Its efficacy verges on magic, and it seems a tool for creation which God forgot inside one of His creatures when He made him."

- Jose Ortega y Gasset (Spanish philosopher and humanist, 1883-1955)

Table of Contents

For my family

For Mommy

For Grandma

For Nanny

For Tomorrow

Soul Searcher

Held in the palm of her hand
Kept close to her like her survival depended on it
Unable to be seen by the common eye
Because one look would freeze ill intentions like Medusa's glare
Guarded by hesitance, protected by caution
Precious jewel given by God and held as the treasure
That would make her life rich
It was written about in stars that twinkled
In eyes guiding ambition through dark times
The image of her, arms clasped, holding on to it
Ready to cast aside any who bear to claim to it
Was folklore in circles of her siblings and friends
Sung in sad ballads of past loves
On the eve of her transformation
The devil cast a spell that trapped her light hidden in tomorrow
And she awoke from youth to discover it gone
Now she's soul searching
Caravan of hope setting out to find her peace
Accompanied by strength, led by intelligence
Sitting in a carriage of personality
On the shoulders of her experiences
Fear hid from elements by sheers woven in resilience
Soul searching
Mapped out across geography
Plotted points of trial and error
Intended to give direction to her future
Set a course of action for her success
Wisdom comes at every stop
And every question asked brings new insight
She finds bits of information in relationships

Short or long, simple or meaningful

Holds on to each like security blankets

Cuddling up in familiar warmth during tough times

I remember her

Beautiful, with the stature of grace

Elegance of fall winds set against leaf shades

And a smile that bore solar on shells with panes

Seeking rays to energize their spirits

I offered to help her find her light

She thanked me for the time spent

Sat and talked today until if faded away

Left me when it came again

So when dawn comes, I turn to my window

Hoping the light over the horizon is her returning to me

Smile wide, light in hand

But when I see it's the sun in the sky

My hope and head falls

And I pray she's closer to her destination

Soul searching

They say that she once sat in a forest of academia

Talked to owls who passed on insight

Read flower beds

Sat against trees tall like buildings

Took tests on bark and moss

All to gain a degree of understanding

Independent, determined, with the will of many

A Princess of mixed moods

Whispers fill bedtime stories

Dinner time conversation

As rumors of her search founds scriptures of persistence

I heard the outcome

As a scribe brought word from over the valley

He said he had great news

His name was E ma EL

I entered the net of his tent

Sat down and logged in to his account of what happened

Found joy with each word

Comfort in knowing the outcome

She found her light

Cast the devil aside and overcame his soldiers

Obstacles led by two generals name trial and tribulation

Reclaimed what was rightfully hers

Was rewarded with what was meant to be

I replied how wonderful

Logged off from his account

Went and wept

Both for her success and the blessing it was

And for death of my morning daydream

Looked out the window

Saw 3 young girls playing

Singing their playtime song

"I've got a light, and I know it's gone shine,

Even if the devil tries to take mine,

Trial and tribulation can try and take that,

Imma reach for my soul and take it right back…"

The lesson of her soul searching lives on

Brown Bag Daddy

My father kept his whole life in a brown bag
Squeezed tight at the top to hold dreams in
Held to his mouth to drown his sorrows
Wash away his pain
Facing tribulation full on liquid courage
He kept his potential in a brown bag
Sin laughed on neighborhood street corners
Wisdom spoken in slurred speech
Young eyes learned that nobody beats the bull
3 dollars for a malt from the ice cream shop
2 for a Schlitz malt liquor bull from the corner store
5 dollar bill from a battered and withered wallet
20 minute walk with your son to the store…priceless
Because a working man works to earn a living
His living was in that brown bag
Not in child support payments
Not in school clothes or school supplies
Not in little league refreshments, basketball shoes, or football cleats
No roses on valentine's days
Only Wild Irish
Because a Mad Dog sees street life with 20/20 vision
But blind to role modeling adolescence
Trapped in a Boones Farm, 40 acres and a mule
Is 40 ounces and a jackass
Pissing away his life, love, and his child's admiration
In park bushes, talking shit as time ticks
And he's hung over like necks hung from nooses
Because responsibility is prejudice against him
Leaving burnt bridges on his lawn
White sheets over his future

Tomorrow is dying

His liver is dying

His spirit is dying

His son is crying

His mother is crying

Optimism is hopeless, no half empty or half full

He sees the world in pints and fifths

Works construction all day

Guzzles lust like a six pack

Six baby mommas, 8 children, no remorse

Heavy hand, smacks brown sistas

Loves brown sugar

Relishes brown bags

In it, he puts everything he has

Don't tell me about heartache and pain, ups and downs

Until you've seen your happiness go at the bottom of a bottle

Come with every open top

Don't talk about obsession, until you wake up and realize you can't stop

When sobriety is worse than insanity

Everyday is better straight up no chaser

When melanin is corroded by wheat and barley

When your first son grows under your nose

And your first love weeps and hardly...

Recognizes you anymore

When the bag you claim, claims you

Your body is bagged, twisted tight like corner store treasure

I can't pour out a little liquor for you

Because I can't stand to have your blood on my hands

Holding on to your grim reaper

When you've run out of time

I sit crying trying to remember the good times

Realizing you didn't leave anything behind

No legacy

No inheritance

No estate

No memories

No wife

No accolades

Just a brown bag and an empty bottle of wine

Brown Bag Daddy

Can I

I want to dry your tears and hold you
Until comfort sets in to your skin like icy hot
And everyone can smell your new day coming
Because your body needs it
Your spirit needs it
Your soul needs it
And he tried too damn hard to take it
Too many times he bossed you around
He insulted you, blamed you, yelled at you
Too many long nights sleeping away the pain
See you never thought it would be like this
When you signed your name on the dotted line
Contracting a disease that you never expected
A disease called H-I-M
A power hungry man who never gave a clue
They usually never do
The two sides of doom
One lulls you in so compassionate, so caring
The other captures you so intense, so angry
It should never be like this
It pains me to know that 1 in 4 women live like this
That fatality comes from the hand of a partner
More than the hand of a stranger
Now you are caught in this web
I want to rub your cheek and sing to you
Songs of a new day
Like Ask Me by Amy Grant
Better Days by Guy Clark
How Come How Long by Babyface
You are Gloria Gainer and you will survive

And if necessary we can be like the Dixie Chicks

Tamper with his black-eyed peas

And run off together leaving a missing person

No on misses at all

You don't deserve it

You are strength

Made it through physical abuse

The constant resistance to losing to a swinging fist

It should never be like this

Your bruised skin is still beautiful

Is a leopard horrific because it has spots?

I make you laugh because I say your complexion has character

But there is no quick healing factor

 And I know you wish for wolverine's claws

To tear through his body of evidence

That says he should get it now

His case stands on brawn

But even in marriage, no is no

You've weathered emotional strain

From isolation to verbal attack

Your will allows you to bounce back

You pinch pennies he overlooks

As he attempts to tighten the purse strings

In this forced incarceration

Times must change

I want to help you plan

Help you store clothes, money, food, and necessities

At my house

Buy tickets out of town on my charge card

Call your family to find the best place for you to escape to

I'll meet you in the back of your job

Take you to social services

Hold your hand when you tell the police to wait

4 days to come get him

So you can execute your escape

I will continue to send you emails

That say one day you will be free

Nothing can steal your sunshine

I promise to be by your side

Because I can't stand to see the situation

But I love to see the wonder in your eyes holding on

Knowing that one day it can come forward

And rule your body once again

An uprising is coming and you will be victorious

I am willing to fight for you

I am willing to strike for you

I am willing to rally for you

I am willing to cry, scream, and shout for you

I am willing to stand for you

Because you are glorious

And it should never be like this

Blood

Blood, sweat and tears
Is like life, beats and rhymes
As I sacrifice my life
Between the paper's lines
As ink flows
High hats and kicks pump inspiration
Like blood vessels and arteries
Nervous system nods notes in neck sways
I breathe in hip hop
And give all that I have
From studios to stages religiously
Giving my only begotten verse
Sacrificed, voice hung on mics
To be resurrected in your memory
Story told in bars of 16
Like scripture written in pro tools
Shrink wrapped and sold to the faithful
I roll with the 4 elements like apostles
Dodging stones of critics
And shackles of the industry
Feeding the hungry with one track
Performing miracles on wax
While people follow the rhythm
Voices recite the lyrics
But most overlook the concept
Boom blast from speakers like organ pipes
Spirits sit in pews, front and back seat car cruising
Churches on chrome
Service begins with key in ignition
Dashboard pulpits send messages

Congregation nods in acceptance looking through tainted glass

I give my revelations to consumers

Those waiting for the signs of apocalypse

When commercial and underground wage war

White robes are jerseys

That chronicle disciples to this society's system

Crowns are fitted

Our new era is marked with logos

I give my devotion to commodity

And yes yes y'all my ten commandments

Jobe my producer to see if he really believes in me

David the egos of neighborhood hyped actors

As I speak to label executive pharaohs

To let my music go

Split minds open at live shows

Turntables like Moses and Aaron

Check 1, check 2

Hope my foolish pride won't Judas my tomorrows

Cuz the taste of fame won't last past the last supper

But the lesson is eternal

I give my trials and tribulations to the love of this culture

So I say give gifts of beat breaks for Christmas

Rhymes caroled in graffiti decorated doorways

DJs built with snow

Write verses for 40 days

From Flash Wednesday to Bambatta Sunday

A Park Jam makes a Good Friday

I dress in track suits and shell toes for all night service on Easter

We search for hidden jewels in songs never forgotten

Our legacy given to disk changers and mp3 players

How many know the definition of a castaway

Past Tom Hanks

Know what it means to be an Outkast

Without any organized noise

My passions can be pictured in the motions of hands side to side

No Mel Gibson to direct my delivery

My call to evangelism is between the faders

And Jesus walks with my entourage

As heads spin at my new testament to skill

I give my life to rock a crowd

My lady waits outside of our empty bed

Like a tomb for me to return home

Gave birth to my freedom with an "I'll always support you"

And cries despair holding on to sheets like a shroud

That can't cover the hole in her heart

Because her sunlight is gone

So she waits 3 days for me to return home

Just to tell her my music needs me to go again

Tell me, what have I lost to gain success?

What have I given to touch your soul?

What does it take to reach my people?

What do I have left when the beat stops?

Just Hip Hop, Hip Hop

I Want

I wanna hold the sun in my hand

Squeeze light beams into ghettoes

Shower the tenements with hope

So that the brightness in young eyes is the shining of their spirit

I wanna whisper winds of promise into the alley ways

So that street residents can be comforted in corrugated homes

I wanna tie hearts together so that love and commitment

Can coexist again

I wanna set individuality free again

So little kids can feel good about what they want to be again

I want beauty to be a given so that everyone can realize it

I want pride to be a byproduct of self discovery

I want to live life to the fullest

Until life doesn't live me anymore

I want my words to inspire and change to be what we're seeking for

I want minds to open and creativity to push through

To the other side of insecurity

Because scared thoughts don't spark thoughts

I want your conscious set ablaze like Colorado forest fires

I want random thoughts to be normal

And well thought insincerity to be weird and unusual

I want my living legacy to be my dying eulogy

My pen's passion to be my love's definition

The instant that changes your life to be this rendition

I want tomorrow's whispers

To be the yells of yesterday

So that progress fades out like your favorite song

Change comes next

I want hearts to beat to the cadence of my poems

So that I can write the songs that make the whole world breathe

I want smiles to be popular

Waves brought back like vintage clothing

Head nods as greetings *Gone til November*

Like Wyclef's opportunity at artistic legitimacy

I want toll booths to fight homelessness

Not a booth with a government employee

Just a road block with homeless people and cups

But you have to stop

I want love and sex to switch places

So that I can just fall into it

Be like, "it just happened"

While I would run from sex

Because I need to get myself together first

I want vacations from work to be as long as grade school

I want adult summer camps

In Aruba, Zimbabwe, and Jamaica

I want commuter flights to be public transportation

So jet lag is the only hindrance to long distance relationships

I want music CDs to be reasonable again

Not the price of a concert ticket

Or I'm going to Re-run and Roger these cats like the Doobie Bros.

I want Che shirts to come with an "ignorental" advisory sticker

That says, "Read and article on the man first before you buy this"

I want to see them make BBQ shacks in the south Atkins approved

So that the high blood pressure brigade can march the streets in protest

Like Montgomery or Selma

Because they are taking our carbohydrates

So we don't have the energy to think or run

But Harriet Tubman didn't lead the Underground Railroad

On protein shakes and chittlin, lettuce and tomato wraps

The LA riots wouldn't have lasted as long

On a small chili and a side salad

No disrespect to those who have lost weight

But there is something else we are losing

They just ain't telling us

Their images say you are too fat

Now they say you can't lose that

So somewhere else must be where the problem's at

But that's too complex and I want simplicity

And my happiness to be the most complicated part of my life

Because it comes in so many ways

I want what I want

I don't want it any other way

Blues Traveler

It was a half past sunrise
And the sweat was beating down his face
His shoulders were heavy, but his heart was strong
And inside... his soul had a song
Society was sad and mournful
He was an artist, slave to the word
That picked from his field of thought
And crafted poems that spread across acres of insight
A field hand, whose field hollers,
Told stories that held the power of pride
Legacy of love, and hope in proper cadence
A blues traveler
Who sang songs of prose, played emotions like an instrument
And toe tapped a rhythm that life breathed to
Wrote from the Delta
Not Mississippi, but the place in his spirit
That knew a change was gone come
So his moans were freedom and his hums were battle cries
That signaled a call to action
A blues traveler
Determination made Leadbellies and strong minds
Where Blind Boys were Fuller fight
Hoping to one day see how to B.B. Kings
Tongue was rural like sop biscuits and blackberry molasses,
Hogmaws and neckbones
He knew that his pen stirred metaphors and truth
Together like collards and fatback
His voice had a presence on the mic
Like Ma Rainey had on stage
Articulate minstrel birthing blues dreams like WC Handy

A blues traveler

Bobby Blue, lyrics never Bland

Old soul's hand grasped concepts

And weaved them into tomorrows

Bessie Smith melodies play out slam poems

He's talking wisdom loud like Howlin Wolf Chester Arthur

Called by stages, held by hearts, adored by minds

Taking time to lay their problems on faith

Like notes on black lines

His notebook more than a symphony

More than a concerto

He was a blues traveler

Went from picking in the fields to plucking heart strings

Breathing life into closed minds

Steel hard and cold like harmonicas

Improvising with empty shells

Because America has drunk us dry

But he takes us and plays in a jug band

Taps one foot, spits affirmation across mentals

Gives us us back

A blues traveler

Two steps away from plantations where concepts

Were put to work to pick thoughts

To form the fabric of our lives

Long days to entertain a crowd

So when it's a half past sundown

The house lights raise, the show is finished, his poem is over

His song is done

All that's left is a moan and a hum

She Said

She said

I don't know if I can

I knew that she could

Just didn't know if she would

Wasn't from the hood

But her house was dilapidated

Broken in parts like the whole of her heart

And the struggle for identity was tearing her apart

Her promise and passion was ripped to shreds

And they tend to call her black girl lost

How can she be lost

When she knows where she is

And it's in this purgatory everyday that she lives

So when she spoke those words

I knew they were true

I just didn't know what to do

See I knew the man that paternally made her

And I knew the man that eventually betrayed her

And I knew where believing in manhood would take her

Down a path to illusion

Where she ends up shackled

So I offered a chance to take the road less traveled

She resisted the chance and I didn't understand

She said how can she trust another man's hand?

How could she believe another man's words?

That sank in me deeper than indigestion

This moment where I learned an important lesson

My spirit was left with so many questions

While my manhood and femininity were full of second guessing

I looked into eyes sunk lower than Jesse Jackson's integrity

A well worn face from feigning a fake smile

While her heart burned from man reflux

The pink stuff just made her look like she was all right

But pretty in pink was in a pretty pickle

It was pretty damn obvious

That what I offered

Wasn't salvation for her

It was salvation from my own guilt

She said

I don't know if I can

I knew that she could

Just didn't know if she should

If believing in another man would set her expectations

Higher than tie dye kids popping X at raves

Only to have her hope fall

Further than one hit wonders

Into relative obscurity

Where you can only hang on to the good times

Old school reminisce

But that only brings back the pain

And how could she know I wouldn't bring the same

Mind worn from strain

Rooted in disgust for men

Kunta Kinte battered from carrying these chains

She said

I don't know if I can

I knew that she could

Only if I showed her I understood

No woman should bow down

Only by vote should a king earn his crown

Popular opinion only strokes his ego

But the Electoral College should be her

The council of elders her heart, her spirit, and her wisdom

Passed down from mothers and wives

Who've felt the pain of withered tears

No woman is property

As this society makes beauty a mockery

No woman should live in fear

No man's masculinity should be revered

Because he's yet to learn what it truly is

Men, remember only God can judge

So labeling her is not your right

She doesn't answer to your vision, only God's sight

So concentrate more on learning how to love

So that she can lean on you for a change

She said

I don't know if I can

I said

I don't know if we can either

Curls

My fear unfurls as I get lost in your curls and my soul twirls

In tune to the shades of your beauty

Melodious carols of echoing exquisiteness

I hear the hum of strength and charm in my sleep

Shadowed by day with your lingering impression

I step…no dance a two step all day long

With wondering eyes and silent questions

What the hell is wrong with him?

But I know…….I know

My fear unfurls as I get lost in your curls and my soul twirls

In tune to the shades of your beauty

If the hills are alive with the sound of music

Then the streets are livid with the beat of your royalty

Queen blisters the pavement leaving cracked blacktop

As car horns, people's yells, radio and TVs cry an ode to you

I dance a two step all day long

to whispering voices and befuddled shoulder taps

Is he ok?

But I know…….I know

My fear unfurls as I get lost in your curls and my soul twirls

In tune to the shades of your beauty

Symphony of attitude, orchestra of personality

la la la la la da da di da da da

Life imitating art

My day has become a musical

You are the star

The plot is

My fear unfurls as I get lost in your curls and my soul twrls

In tune to the shades of your beauty

You bad bad thang you!

Bad Day

The sunlight is mad at me for sleeping at night

Saying son, yo, that just ain't right

So of course I got to wake up now

My bank account and my money

Bout to break up now

I wish they'd just make up now

But ok, the situation must be shaken up now

I just gotta think up how

I run the water

But even that don't like me

Even the shower gel wants to fight me

I grab my bath sponge and ask politely

Is it ok if you just wipe me?

So now the temperature changes constantly

Because the hot and cold water enjoys mocking me

I'm like could y'all quit playing possibly

So that I can lather and bathe properly?

Obviously, it seems a mockery

That I'm arguing with inanimate property

But today is just one of those days

So now I must brush my teeth

But my toothbrush done hid

The toothpaste is fussing

Saying I lost her lid

So now she's all dried out

Sobbed and sighed all out

Saying "You don't love me, you wanna squeeze my insides out!"

My brush is conspiring

It's really getting tiring

Because my edgers he's contemplating hiring

A little mishap when I'm trying to line and

Make a close fade an option worth vying with

Lazy sun of a gun, what them bristles is for

Didn't like the question hated me even more

So he hollered at my razor, said "Get him extra clean"

So the aftershave will give me a little extra sting

I'm a victim in my own house and I see impending doom

And the funny thing is... I ain't even left my room

Ready to depart, got my clothes to play their part

But couldn't get my breakfast to provide any spark

Fridge like "who goes there?" without the ark

I'm like it's me yo and he said "I don't know no me yo"

The freezer was like "It ain't nobody that we know"

Allright that's cool, go head front on me yo

I'm bout to leave, because this is what I don't need yo

Out the front door, attitude kinda stank

My Honda took offense, man it wouldn't even crank

Baby baby, not this morning work with me

Took a whole lot of persuasion and coercion

Told her I'd park her beside a Suburban or Excursion

I got to my job, and nobody would speak to me

Even the elevator doors closed kinda weak to me

Got to my cubicle and my chair had a real stank squeak to me

My radio on my desk wouldn't get the right frequency

My keyboard keys felt like they didn't love me

Even my monitor looked a little fuzzy

My boss never came by, my coworkers had no convo

The mail guy just sailed by

Like "I'll bring you some mail tomorrow!"

My phone never rang, voicemail light never lit

My administrative assistant called this morning and quit

My insurance agent called, automotive and medical
Trying to recall the dialogue still in a daze
I swear he said the monthly fee on the policies got raised
The doctor called to tell what my x-ray had shown
Couldn't believe it, the x-ray said I had no bones
I said how is that possible on an x-ray of the chest?
Even that machine didn't like me, staged a protest
So now I gotta go again, he said "Tomorrow at 10"
I said ok doc, he said "Ok son I'll see you then"
And with enemies like these I don't really need friends
All I know is that I wish that this whole day would end

I called my homeboy to tell 'em what was going on
But for some reason my homeboy was gone
So then I proceeded to call him at home
He answered, but I could tell he wasn't alone
I said what up, he said "What up"
I'm like what is the deal?
"A little under the weather man", I knew the lie wasn't real
Because right after that I heard a woman's squeal
So once again I asked yo dog what's the deal?
He coughed and was like "Nothing", I said don't lie to me
Who's the shorty in the back?
He said "It's the TV"
She said "Hang up the phone, come back to me"
The voice really sounded so familiar to me
For the life of me I wondered who it could be.
Obviously somebody wrong because he's lying to me
I said take care dog as caring as could be
Got my keys, because this I was dying to see
Rolled to my boy's house, sly as can be
Noticed his car and a black and grey Infinity

Sorta looked like my...nah it couldn't be

Sorta like my girlfriend's q45 to me

Went to the door knocked hard as could be

Couldn't believe this was happening to me

He came to the door as startled as could be

I pushed past him and ran into the house to see

Into his bedroom, female as naked as could be

Fine as hell but completely a stranger to me

I apologized as my man looked angrily at me

He said "Come 'on dog is that what you think of me?"

I said man it's been a day you wouldn't believe

And even my mind is playing tricks on me

Star Baby

She was a star baby
Bright light beamed in the delivery room when she was born
Glow like whispering willows on a bright summer day
Cries sounded like blue jays humming soul tunes
But I know that when winter comes souls diminish
Stars don't shine
The mist of confusion is thick because we exhale our pain
Then try and suck in what little optimism is left
To warm our spirits
And a star baby cries frozen tears
And I write cold words
That won't score well or set well
But the well has run dry on entertainment value
Because my journal has become a morgue
Filled with potential lost too soon
I spend hours on autopsies
But you can't edit reality
So the poem lays; a cold slab of perception
And I want to breathe life back into her
That little star baby
Her light is needed, her shine brings tomorrow
I'm tired of walking around in yesterday
So I pray that the season passes fast
My pen still pissing away imagination
Words are cold and harsh like winter winds
I draw snow angels in margins to guard my meaning
And throw snow balls at trash cans in frustration
Over ideas that won't come
Wear black under my clothes everyday
In mourning for that little star baby

A star baby who loses her life when the temperature drops

When they don't classify it as hot no more

I call myself a Jedi

Not because of skill, but because I'm forced to write the truth

And will it into the minds of strangers

Binding U-N-I verse by verse

But can you see the death star

The dark side of the page is the side you write your fear on

I fear that spring will come

She won't come back

That little star baby

Glow like whispering willows on a bright summer day

Laugh sounding like blue jays humming soul tunes

Skin enriched with a shade of melanin

Rich like blackberry molasses

A star baby

Firefly that captured seraphim in the playground of her mind

Wrote poetic lullabies on tree bark in honeydew

Danced jigs with grasshoppers to the cadence of woodpeckers

Lit hillsides with her smile

A muse that my mind misses in winter

That you never clap for, you never cheer,

Cast from rounds eliminating the last on the path to acceptance

A star baby

Pens

The pot of gold at the end of the rainbow
Is promise at the end of realization
But if you never realize your potential
Then promise is just a passing possibility
As thieves rob temples of prose
Pushing pen princes to cry tears of purple rain
As their Morris days pass with time
They tend to call my cries alliterate
As Promise Rots In Systems Oppressing peNs
And people put it off as passing fancy
My passion to put truth to paper
Makes me a possible pawn
Or a target of this predatory practice
When alliteration isn't a poetic device
But a device of power mongers
Who repeat the same cycle with the same black faces
Our pens are being incarcerated
You can say you know why the caged bird sings
But I know why the caged bird cries
Until the ink runs dry
Our souls are stained in shame
We watch it
As newborns are slated for a cell and a number
Not a pencil and a journal
Like pre-ordered burial plots
It's only a matter of time
It's been *28 days* and I can see the living dead
Infected with a *Resident Evil*
They are snatching our leaders and locking them away
Hung by their larynx

Chained and shackled at the mind

Now every fall we wonder why the rain falls longer now

Tears fall stronger now

Sentences run longer now

We walk blind to the fact, but some know

As fiends tap veins to inject black ink back into their pens

So they can write their pain away

Poems that only get read at visiting hours

Verses with no DJ, only a CO

Their label isn't Def Jam, it is habitual felon

Some are eventually sent on work release

Just look how they work

As young pens wear prison gear, tattoo prison tears

And live imprisoned lives outside of prison walls

That only makes the transition easier

Promise Rots Inside Systems Oppressing peNs

And OZ remains one of our favorite TV shows

As though we forgot the wizard was a lie

They had what they needed all along

But the wicked witch of the east signs acts

That wage war on pens

And didn't get crushed when the towers fell

No we are not in Kansas anymore

But in a facility called correctional

But white out just covers, it doesn't erase

As poems sit in cells like pages of a chapbook

Only to be read at visiting hours

Their sentences run on

People want to look and call them inmates

I say look and see where most of our poets have gone

Metaphor

From the depths of me
My emotions peek out to see if you're there
Because that's where they hide
You go get it
After counting to 23
Strawberry letter written to our tomorrow
The smell leads like Martin Lawrence to window sill apple pie
This is our life
I want it to last longer than pre-pubescent orgasms
Hold me in your middle passage
Where too many men have jumped ship to escape
Drowning in the wet of your midnight tears
I want to be your slave
Work the field of your mind state
Pick picnic baskets full of understanding
That we can weave into the fabric of happiness
Share in the crop
For too long I've sent Trojan horses
Into castles with false pretenses to attack caring souls
But see love doesn't live here anymore (in my crotch)
A heart is a house for love and you hold the keys
As my head spins at the thought of you
Like cassette tapes, movie reels
My popular culture
Club and love like this is Nuveau
Lean on me and sing our love's song
Melodies in major and minor scales
Roller coaster ride Paramount to lasting memories
Past amusement in your Bush Gardens
Some claim as a King's Dominion

Bright light set against a dark night, Heaven's constellation

I want to pour you into the dipper

So I can drink from your soul

Be filled by your presence

I want you to be so much a part of me

That I feel I lose a part of you when I clip my toenails

My foundation is stone frozen by Medusa's glare

The beauty of your locks long and deep rooted

Like our history

Our love

Old school like Ashford and Simpson, Rick James and Tina Marie

Round and round like vinyl records

We spin a cocoon for our love to mature

Fly free flapping like Butterfly wings

Colors hue

Rainbows leading me to the pot of gold

I follow home from work to you

Trek into the stars of your eyes

Into deep space where our relationship's 9 lives

Guarantee immortality

Highlanders in this social society

Coming together to fight temptation

Feeling the rush of the quickening

There can be only one

Too

Many ways to describe our love in similes

Two love struck entities

Lost my head over you

Tongue sword, so sharp

Cut into my heart when you said "I love you to"

I am your poet

And you are my metaphor

Homicidal Maniac

I am a homicidal maniac
And I can't stop the killing
Cold and calculated
Able to murder paper with well swung strokes
Abstract psychopath
With a lust for applause
It feeds me

I am a homicidal maniac
My murder weapon is sharp
Leaving drips of eloquence
So that forensics knows I wrote the crime
This is the product of a calculating mind
I can't be stopped

So call Harrison Ford, Clint Eastwood, Denzel, Bruce Willis
Or Samuel L. Jackson
It won't stop me
I'll still take shots at minds
Assassinating ignorance
I'll kidnap attention and hold it for my satisfaction
Leave poems floating in the water wet of your subconscious

I am a homicidal maniac
And I can't stop the killing
This is not *Virtuosity*, *Sam I Am*, *Hannibal*, or *7 Deadly Sins*
Because I am smarter than all of those put together
Check my work
From sonnets to limericks
Carefully carved out of my creativity

I won't see *Law and Order*

Unless it's *SVU*, because Ice T's an OG and he know how I gets down

I'm leaving letters with newspaper clippings

Cut words forming haikus

As clues

Those that have witnessed my work

The police have reached

As notebooks and PCs are put into witness protection

I am a homicidal maniac

Words are scared

The police are desperate

They send a hip hop producer

Out on the street as *Bait*

Saying he knows where the money is

So I seek his tracks as a map

To where the money's at

I am a homicidal maniac

And I can't stop the killing

I know they are after me

We are way past conspiracy theories

In my secret basement

I have pictures of venues on my walls...

AND I LOVE EVERY ONE

I am a homicidal maniac

One of the *Usual Suspects*

As I leave the captains office

He tries to figure why the name on the open mic lists

Reads PM

Walking out the door to my ride

The carpel tunnel in my wrists seems to go away instantly

I wave goodbye to the station

The captain reaches for his pen and it all comes clear

"Pppp...Papermate!"

I am a homicidal maniac

And I can't stop the killing

I need to control the words

I need to use the words

I only exist because of the words

I must kill microphones, stages, and pages

I am a homicidal maniac

I can't stop the killing

Deep in thought

I want to write until my pen bleeds

Until my hand shakes and trembles

With the pressure of wisdom and overstanding

I want to have an epiphany

Have it pound my skull so hard

My scalp expands and contracts

I want to realize an insightful thought

That comes from so deep

That my penis grows, my chest heaves and my toes curl

From the orgasm of passionate wordplay

I will call my momma and tell her I love words

And I'll bring my poem home for thanksgiving dinner

I want eternity

Connected to words like Siamese twins

But the industry carries a scalpel

We share one heart

So I worry that they'll take the poem and leave me listless

Because dead poets get better promotion

I want to write until my eyes hurt

From looking at dim lit paper

Sitting in the darkness of my subconscious

Hoping the light-bulb comes through

But I'm bright idealess

I'm trying to answer the call of this blessing

Cascading dark brooding concepts breathing heavily in my ear

I hang up

They call again

I call 911; they arrest and take away my resistance

So I write

The emancipation proclamation Lincoln should've recited

The new deal Roosevelt should've proposed

Speeches Al and Jesse need to give

The accounts the NAACP's Crisis needs to report

As exciting as the front page of the enquirer

Attacking people's misconceptions

The conspiracy theories they subscribe to

About whether their neighbor is a communist, terrorist, drug kingpin, clone,

Black radical, or militarist

From fear to modern day McCarthyism

I want couplets and sonnets to massage and caress me

Not feel like a misogynist

As my muse nurtures my creativity

Like black women nurse broken men's egos

I want to write until my soles are coarse and hard

From running across rough terrain

Because street cats got cerebrum like the Sahara

Dry

I want to rain conscious thought

Until their soul is drenched in promise

Til their minds are flooded with critical analysis

I write for patriarchy

I'm a Black male, healthy and educated

What the hell do you think they taught me to do?

So I write for freedom

But only read it where they open their doors

Damn

I want to write until the US government represents my community

Then I will write until popular opinion is weighed against social responsibility

Then we can choose who won by majority selection

But we'll still be counting votes

I want to write until they discover I have turrets

That my uncontrollable sentence structure is relentless

And you keep trying to slip Prozac in my water

Because my ADD affects how long I listen to your bullshit

I want to write until change comes

Until retribution comes

Until equality comes

But the frustration of this desire to craft the perfect prose

Has made me impotent

And Viagra can't help the writers block

When putting these words together the right way

Can't get any harder

And it really isn't funny

I want to create my living legacy

Finally recognizing it's my life long dedication to write

Until I am a historical monument

So can I get that grant check in the mail?

Because capitalism created starving artists

Survival requires compensation

Past the satisfaction of my spirit

But I just try to write my fortune

With vowels and consonants

As legal tender

With my journal as a wallet

Flashing pages like old sugar daddies flash money clips

Seeking the admiration of my peers

And the adoration of vibrant youth

I am my own worst critic

So I wait until the producers of this show

Write the final episode

Last breath spoken, last word wrote

And my lungs no longer on the air

Crack Baby Serenade

Tomorrow was always further away than
The trails of one tear down his cheek
So when they said to reach for his future
He just retreated and cried
Water welled up inside
It was like his dreams were drowning in his eyes
They said *Hope Floats*
But he believed that happy endings only happened in movies
Hero isn't what you're called when you're Sandra Bullock homely
So tell me what he is supposed to do
When life is just a lie that gets fed up even worse
What he's going through isn't just fit for anyone
It's mayhem on steroids
This sullen soul doesn't know the price of happy
But he knows they give sad free to the po, broke and lonely
And throw wishes into the water to learn how to swim
But it's different strokes for different folks
Can't breast stroke when your chest is sunken
Can't back stroke when it's weighed heavy
Butterflies are beautiful
But the last time he felt that way
Was when he was in his mother's arms at the hospital
Before social services took him away
Can't fly with undeveloped wings
Can't swim with inoperable limbs
He runs a butter knife across his wrists
As committed to suicide as this world is committed to nurturing his tomorrows
You tell a crack baby that is just means a rose made it through the concrete
That making it in this world isn't as hard as it seems

That the title is just a premonition of his breakthrough

And white lies are purely sincere

But white rock put him here

Future taking its last breathe in his tears

Momma may have, Poppa may have

But God bless the child with residue in his veins

Because he never asked to have his own

Never asked for this foster home

Blue blooded family raising a white-blooded teen

In this distorted illusion of the American dream

He begs Death to come knock on his door

Come claim him as he wanted his mother to do

Realizes that even if it was her it would feel the same

He's sitting in darkness

Arms holding the last bit of sanity he has left

He will no longer face blind judgment

Because justice can't see he is at the end of his rope

Societal norms picnicking at the sight of this strange fruit

Hanging from the tree of knowledge that this world doesn't love him

No foundation beneath him only a noose above him

Wool pulled over his eyes, but his dreams still tug him

Wishes he had a manuscript on how this spade could win freedom

Won't bid on trying with no books, only possibles

Big and little joker leaving him set as forgotten

Left behind in negative impressions

He didn't ask for it, now he asks for it to end

Picks up a pen...stabs it into his skin

He wants to write his eulogy

Wonders if this is how his mother and father wrote his destiny

Only the ink never dried it flows in his veins

Never writes love stories, funny anecdotes, only pain

Wishes the tears would stop falling

Sad words dancing in the rain

Leaving his journal stained

Believes he is so worthless that Death doesn't even know his name

He's in darkness

Holding on to the last bit of sanity he has left

His only wish is to die

But all he can do is cry

And all I can offer him...

Is this Crack Baby Serenade

Margins (inspired by C.P. Maze)

I sometimes wish I could write stars that fall in tears

So that you could cry me a constellation

And people would marvel at the beauty of my words

Define lives by their existence like astrology

But aspiration can be an asylum

Where walls of affirmation can have me trapped

Trying to plot my way to significance

I don't reside there

I reside in the margins, on the edge

One step from insanity or revelation, lunacy or genius

It all depends on what's in between

I exist where pipsqueaks aren't chicken

They're souls weighed down by burdens until they're too weak to speak

Cast off like dirty linen

But you can't wash away the pain

I let the wretched residue wet my pen and I wail away at indignity

Write my corrections in blood

In the margins

One inch all around like the one percent wall around wealth

I exist where holes are on the left

Which explains why revolution and reform is so far away

Where lines are college ruled instead of picket lines

I take notes for future books and papers

Etch daydreams and doodle freedom

Spend time trying to comprehend one extreme or the other

On the outside of common understanding

I exist in the margins

A pocket of potential where reflection can arrive

And hindsight can leave a mark of discovery

Where you can read for proof and edit the misconceptions

You can find me where things don't seem to fit
But so much can be said
Change is normal here
Rebellion is normal here
Freedom is normal here
In the margins

Vocabulary pt. 1

Granddaddy always said that family should be <u>uniform</u>
So he couldn't wait for the day he got his uniform
<u>Homogenous</u> loyalty was the code
So similar skin found similar sins in the midst of their souls
<u>Presumptuous</u> and proud
Believed <u>valor</u> guaranteed victory
So they fought for the hell of it
Spoils of war, glory was <u>rancid</u>
He lusted for the smell of it
Rules were <u>stringent</u>, discipline was the key
Unlocked potential
So they trained
Strong body, strong mind
Read, re-arranged time
Because judgment was to be swift
He never said much
A little embarrassed of his lisp
But his spirit spoke <u>eradication</u>
Oppression and injustice on his list
There truly were guerillas in the mist
The Angels heaven missed
Who fell into a stint like this
A stretch where pain and suffering exists
He <u>standardized</u> his tears
They <u>conformed</u> to a strict law
Most never made it down his jaw
He was a rebel

Objective Correlative pt. 1

They held hands like past loves hold resentment

Ancestry woven together

Quilted into devotion

This park was a haven

Their eden

Where forbidden fruit were doctor visits

And they chose not to eat

From the tree of knowledge

Test results slithering into their happiness

Young eyes gleefully admiring the view

Wise eyes admiring his strength

They say don't look a gift horse in the mouth

But Mabel's daughter was mule headed

So they decided to play it low key

And take the grandiose out of parenting

So their house became Harlem

Sugar shack kisses placed on the forehead

Of a blessing 16 months on this earth

Cotton club caresses when the pain was too much

Because his cells were Russian

Hammering his health, slicing his vibrancy

These 3 wise folks…two elders and the Holy Spirit

Traveled the path to nurturing

To discover this star

Hump day was when the weight was lifted

They could rest in the delight the young one brought

Without worry, without concern

And see his innocence blossom like the spring flowers

That surrounded them

Frank was an angel Mabel thought

Able to accept a responsibility not his
Saw that this young boy's blood wasn't his
But it wasn't a concern
So instead of promising a ceremony and a ring
He promised to bind this family together
And keep sad ceremonies at bay

Vocabulary pt. 2

She wished she had abstained
They told her attention was addictive
And he gave it in large doses
So she soaked in his benevolence
Said it felt like heaven
Kept faith in his reverence
Until the angel fell from grace
And a devil lay next to her
Jealousy and arrogance were prevalent
He believed her his property
She held dissent from that approach
Sought to remove the noose around her throat
Hung on his every move
She aspired for college
He aspired to be known
In the streets he made his home
Until one night his charisma planted a seed
9 months later it had grown
Affiliated with the wind
He was gone in a breeze
Her contemporaries told her he would do so
She didn't want to believe so
Still cold from the breeze of the swinging do'
Pregnancy her only diversion from the loneliness
She came to live with this truth
It was evident that her life would be changed forever
His absence was evidence her friends were right
But the new baby girl would be the proof

Hybrid Theory (for the girl who loved "hybrid music")
Based on lyrics from *I Used to Love Her* by Common

I met this girl when I was ten years old
And what I loved most she had so much soul
Intelligent, loved to read hearts and comprehend emotions
Studied English and lived honest
She was Sublime, and I took in her charm like second hand smoke
She had me tipsy, my "40 oz. to Freedom"
I escaped in our conversations
We met everyday at Linkin Park
On a "Collision Course" to debate
Her analysis of today's society, my passion for Hip Hop
I talked of my first tape, my first rhyme
She talked of the first time it turned its back on her
See she listened to Hybrid Music
Found a place of comfort where rhymes seduced a rock beat
Her passion was for an alternative
Where objectification wasn't Common
She needed to create a new place where music made Sense
She grew and found purpose
The mirror image in the songs never changed
So she cracked the mirror and left that bad luck where it lay
That was good for her, she was becoming well rounded
I thought it was dope how she was on that freestyle shit
So we met to talk every day at 311
I planned for it with anticipation, my "Way From Chaos"
I felt that she was an "Evolver", shape shifter who morphed a new compromise
I just wished I could hold her in my arms and head nod for one moment
Let the boom bap be our bop
Renaissance our culture's definition like Harlem
See she listened to Hybrid music

Felt it was her Rage Against The Machine, and as funny as it seems

It was her idea of reform to seek a new understanding outside of the norm

I told her that Hip Hop found sanctity in punk clubs

She said Aces High didn't suit her

Because they sought diamonds before hearts

I guess it was in the cards

About my people she was teaching me

By not preaching to me, but speaking to me

In a method that was leisurely, so easily I approached

She dug my rap, that's how we got close

We talked, everyday at 311 in Linkin Park

While Gorillaz in suits swung from corporate vines

In a Crazy Town, cats "Suburb Thuggin"

What's a mansion in the hills?

An asylum or a battered women's shelter?

I thought about the question she posed

I said it depends on whether the party is full

Of men with broken egos or women with broken spirits

Of course my Hip Hop still speaks with her native tongue

Says "Arrest the President", casts "Reasonable Doubt",

Tells me that "I Am"

She asked me if they were so "Ready to Die" how long before "The Massacre"

9 years…damn

She listened to hybrid music

Said a man who carries a gun but no compassion

Carries a Limp Biskit, owes a debt Payable On Death

I respected her, shit hit me in the heart

Plugged me into a new way of thinking

Like Herc did those speakers in the park

She was there for me, I was there for her

Pull out a chair for her, turn on the air for her

And just cool, cool out and listen to her

Hope that what I love could be what she loved about me

A chance to touch what meant so much before

A "Resurrection" inside of her

Where she could B-girl and I could B-boy

But she had to "Go" and I let her

Eventually if it was meant to be, then it would be

Because we related, physically and mentally

I don't know if I reminded her of a time before strength or consciousness

Maybe it was my looking glass eyes and she couldn't shatter hope again

She stopped showing up at 311, at Linkin Park, in Crazy Town

I'd sit on a bench and reminisce, think about our conversations

She was fun then, I'd be geeked when she come around

Now I sit here with my CD player

Push play on the new Quarashi album, let the tears run down my face

No head nod to stop the pain, I reminisce

Original, pure untampered and down sister

Boy I tell ya, I miss her

Rashna (misspelled gratitude)

Paris in springtime

The view from the beach looking out over the Arabian Sea

The Rain Forests of Costa Rica

Images of things existing but yet unseen

In my life, at this juncture

It seems that I am caught between the seams

The joining of two hands on a night

Where dinner and conversation meet perfectly

The origin of our meeting tells perfectly

A cute story of drinks, anecdotes, and taxes

Strange as that mix may seem

It painted an amazing scene

Like the hand of God that Picasso'd that cute face

Commissioned Rodin to sculpt a voluptuous figure

Put it perfectly in place

Ansel Adams wouldn't have captured a better picture

Of style and grace

But I digress

Or rather impress to you that you can hear how wonderful something is

See the beauty in it but never come closer than your imagination

That's where her heart is

A cool breeze, vividly colored leaves

Sand near a clear blue sea

Distinct species of strength in tall bellowing trees

I spent hours negotiating travel arrangements

Hoping to outlast the no dating decree

A special time when men could stay gone

But women and children fly free

No flights to far away intimacy available for me

Because plane-ly, flying high hit real low last time

So now this vessel is grounded

I sat at check in and blew kisses to text messages

Hope missing like vowels in shorthand

Some call her an Angel

Bring her flowers on the 18th day of the month

Find rejuvenation in her smile

I called her often

Planted seeds of hope in my conscious

Found rejection in her silence

They say that truth hurts

So when you're named it

Does it mean you are hard to handle

Or will hardly ever be handled again

I debate that with my foolish male pride

Let my understanding come play outside

They say you can't look at the sun, you'll go blind

So why do I expect her to bare her soul

I won't cover myself in anger

No sun block to escape from my ignorance

I can never know her life or her reality

Angels can't please everybody

I am no better than any other

Unless I prove myself so

I can only use seconds to make myself worthy

Just the time it takes for her to say hello

This is my symphony of incoherent thoughts

My Beethoven's rant

I wish that I could stop but I can't

So I stand ready to battle

Hoping to overwhelm my insecurities

Too many men seek to overwhelm her sensibilities

Like Alexander invading Persia

I can't control it

I can't explain it

I can't analyze it

I wonder if my inadequacy is because I'm clueless

Or still frozen in the memory of when she cared what my voice sounded like

I talk randomly to no one like I have turrets

Not wanting to waste the words I would give to her

Hoping that the wind will take them to her

My passport picture is a frown

Because I know I may never truly see the beauty of that foreign land

Like…

Paris in springtime

The view from the beach looking out over the Arabian Sea

Or the Rain Forest of Costa Rica

Never rest my head there

Never take pictures of happy moments there

This isn't love…it is respect

For a woman whose name means more than the work of most

Whose life would drive some over the brink

Whose will and strength can't be measured

God, tell me she can be guarded

So she doesn't have to justify her actions

Or better yet, tell me she doesn't have to be bothered at all

So I can stop worrying if she thinks about my stupidity

Tell me to stop rambling

About a woman who I have only been around a few times

Talked to for only a few weeks

And will never forget

Nanny's Soliloquy

I love you

Is all that I can muster up to say

So with a Godfather's kiss

I turn my head to hide tears I don't want to fall

Because your eyes seem to be looking home

Past the confines of this hospital bed

See freedom is an oxymoron

That contradicts what's not there

When your strength leaves, your health leaves, your hope leaves

All you can do is lie there

In white sheets like Angels wings

Staring at Peter's gates

For a glimpse of Granddaddy's face

My Nanny

Our family's matriarch

Our north star slowly decaying

I don't want the darkness to take you

Moments are all I can stand

When each touch of your hand cripples my spirit

The same way that this illness cripples your body

I wish I could hold on to all you've ever been to me

Can you tell me how to watch a diva fall?

When VH1 doesn't care about the story

I replay memories like home movies

From the first big pickle you bought me

To weekend excursions to your favorite shopping spots

Cooking that fed more than my hunger

Wise words spoken between sips of wine

Sips that circled like vultures

Until they could pick at your happiness

Help me hold on to my Grandmother

Help me hold onto my sanity

So I can stop sending wishes

Written in invisible ink

Tied to the legs of birds with broken wings

Who can't fly their way home

My love pigeon holed between my fears

And my cowardice

Send me a Sunday morning sermon

Tithe me 10% of the time she spent

Ushering people's faith

Pray that I find the strength to say goodbye

So that I can savor every day she gets

Please Nanny...rebel

Push this sickness on an exodus like refugees

Paul our tomorrow

Our connection will be a Hotel Rwanda

And I will protect it with all that I have

Whatever I can offer

God I say to you now

Take this poem as a token

Protect the life she has left

Give her the ticks of a clock only you can read

I will speak this poem

Whenever, wherever

Until the day my pen's worth

Becomes her eulogy

Take it and take me

Use it as you will

My grasp on this piece

Is my available sacrifice

Because I will never let that woman go

Quoted

Neruda said...

"We have lost even this twighlight. No one saw us this evening hand in hand
   while the blue night dropped on the world."

In the dead of night my blues song

Resonates off the strings of harpies

Playing our love's death kneel

Personalities prepare to defend themselves like titans

A coliseum called a relationship

Where intruding eyes can't remember our last embrace

Can't wait for our next argument

I can't love like this

Baraka said...

"We want to be happy, neglecting to check the definition."

I never looked it up

Never studied its correct use or context

Just cheated and watched your actions for an understanding

But the movie version is never like the book

I didn't really want to know

The whole of you

So I read good days like cliff notes

And to some degree

I graduated to a semblance of a lover

But a bachelor's grasp is only a start

A master's allows you to teach

But a doctorate allows you to gain tenure

Where was my dedication to learning

I just can't love like this

But Ginsberg said...

"How many mornings to be or not to be?"

I don't know the answer

But I know that a warm embrace to greet me

Makes me forget there was a question to be answered

Tell me I'm foolish

Because I don't know the definition of happy

I can give you the root of alone

As I hear Ginsberg ask...

"How many years lie alone in bed and stroke my cock?"

Self-gratification isn't a synonym for joy

See I can't love like this

I can't be like this

Until my commitment

Learns the definition of resilience

Until my arms can learn to let go

As quickly as they hold

Then I know you are here because you want to be

If I can speak the same breath into our hopes

That I do into these poems

If I can reach to you love

With the same hand I grab this pen

Trying to heal these society inflicted wounds

If our photo album

Reads better than a store bought magazine

If your voice stands my hairs

Before it erects my penis

If announcing our relationship is like a playoff game

Then I can truly love like this

Something

There was something about the way she sang a song
It was like the words came to life and danced in front of you
Rebel songs, proud songs, freedom songs
Notes marched faster than we did that morning
On our way downtown with determination on our faces
Warmth in our hearts and pain in our spirit
We held hands not because of solidarity
We held hands because the power of her voice was so strong
We needed to hold to each other up
I clenched the hand next to me tight
As I closed my eyes and followed the Angels
Flying wings of harmony out of the mouth of a blessing
She was vintage
Mainly because she was adept at thrift store lore
Adidas sambas never carried so much importance
Black with stripes colored red, yellow, and green by sharpie
No gym needed, body was strong
The Che wrist band she wore seemed to scream
With the power contained in wrists that
Wrote letters, petitions, poems, editorials, and inspiration
Held a fist high like Thor held a hammer

There was something about the way she smiled
Whenever she was faced with ignorance
Whenever they told her to turn back and go home
Go home?
Can you tell the wind to turn back?
Can you tell the sun to shine, night to fade?
Mother Nature breathed existence into this budding seed
God crafted her blossom from the earth

She was forever natural
No labels could identify her
Her name was its own brand of fly

There was something in the way she stood
Strong and firm
Tank top showed the tenseness of muscles
Truck stop shades hid weary eyes
Lips fuller than Don Cheadle's resume
Chewed blades of grass like a southern belle
Taught backwoods bamas
That Daisy Mae ain't the only hazard
She tattooed a tree on her back
Because the roots of our struggle were buried there
Carried like our tomorrow depended on it
Our beloved
As rich as Oprah
But her wealth was in admiration
Her dedication was to spirits colored purple
Battered and bruised
So as Harpo sits in an Oval office
Dances our lives away in juke joint cabinets
She laughs
Because she's home
Right here on these front lines
I would follow her anywhere
She named the place and time
I'd paint my protest sign on my body
Like avid sports fans
Tailgate outside the building
With 100% fruit juice, grilled tofu burgers, and organic buns
Camp out the night before

To be the first in line to hold the banner with her

Mesmerized by the glare of soul searching eyes

Beaming bright so I sun block my ignorance with Google searches

Research for my health

Wear the term activist like tattooed prison tears

Like I worked for that shit

There was something about her

I fell in love with everything she is

So I sing love songs with bull horns

March to the cadence of freedom

Holding the movement close to my heart

The Reason

I watched him from the edge of the park

Saw him pick up a four leaf clover

And I wondered what the future would hold

Because green plants a lust for capital

I couldn't imagine the system eating another one

Punch a clock, but can't fight for freedom

Reach for wealth, but can't hold on to compassion

Or would he have the luck of the Irish

Take arms, run into the streets,

Speak loud, fight long, and die free

Find a pot of gold at the end of the rainbow

When nations rally, gender falls

Will, wisdom, and devotion are given like 3 wishes

Now…as my daydreams have me taking his innocence

He skips across green grass

Laughs a laugh that reminds me of CNN

Where conservatives bellow ignorant chuckles

Like that child knows no heartache

They know no shame

Where companions are called Franklins and Benjamins

Poor people have no name

A child plays

Held upright by God's hands

Clinging to that four leaf clover

Happy at his discovery with hope in his heart

Because old wives tales say they make wishes come true

No, old wives make wishes come true

Because they birth tomorrow, nurture today, and heal yesterday

Feed us truth

Wash our spirits, hang our tear soaked faces

On their shoulders to dry

This young man waves at his mother

And I hope that when he waves goodbye

It's off to college and not off to war

When his momma will turn scrapbooks

Cry with fingers reading pictures like Braille

Faith in that book like scripture

Heart skips a beat when she gets to his first four leaf clover

Wishes he was home

She opens up her arms for him

But he runs

The field has no enemy fire, no bombs

Only the wind as his Kevlar

Butterflies, not jets over his head

Smile on his face

Feet moving, but the ground is solid

He falls on his bottom but not in

Earthquake doesn't claim him

Flood doesn't take him

Gunshots don't riddle him

Handcuffs don't hold him

Money doesn't make him

Masculinity hasn't shaped him

I watch him and pray for the world

He runs over, looks me in the eyes

Says, "Daddy, look what I got!"

I kiss him on the forehead, stiffen a the car horn

Check for the gun in the small of my back

Grab my backpack, wipe his mother's tears

Tell her to tell him his daddy fought till his last breath

To leave him in innocence

Hope that when he sees me on CNN

He won't believe in my guilt but my innocence

This is for you my son

I pick up a piece of cold steel

Spin the chamber and wish I didn't have to do it this way

You are my revolution

And this is the only means I know necessary

To protect your right to play

So I pray

What when you pick your next four leaf clover

Your wish won't be to have your daddy back

And they never take that innocence away

Defining Moment

See, people find their defining moment in a number of circumstances
But he found his
Where feet move to the rhythm of acceptance
Bodies glide like a summer breeze
Cool, smooth
It doesn't matter what the day holds
Because the nights calm led him to excitement
For a modest entry fee a college boy
Can be so much more
See life was mapped differently on the dance floor
With each agreeing hand, invitation accepted
He danced with wit, intelligence, beauty, charm, strength
Learned to speak a language only bodies can verse
Took special precaution with his grammar
Accented sentences with proper punctuation
Tried not to curse
It was deliverance from shy
Sanctuary from insecurities
You'd lose your mask in the sound
Let the movement free the real you
Never having to stand alone
Because the beat is unifying, electrifying
He found he worked it well
As if the words he couldn't speak out loud
Were written in the air around him
She could read his heart
He danced like free don't come always
A slave to the pulsating passion
Remembered every partner by how they made him feel
Moving in sync like voices singing Negro spirituals

With a lot of soul

It was on that floor that he felt he belonged

That she belonged next to him

A motion picture with its own special soundtrack

Yes, people find their defining moment in a number of circumstances

He found his in a memory

Unexpected, but monumental

The words stay with him like a favorite tune

Replays comfort like home sickness

She simply said, "I remember dancing with you"

Not even knowing that she had met the truth in him

Had seen the God in him

The part of him that grew into a pens worth

Now fingers dance on pages with pens

So as she listens to his poetry this night

The cycle completes and she has experienced

The whole of him

Many nights spent on an underground railroad

Between the wallflowers and DJ booth

On a path to understanding up north

Age has slowed his feet, quickened his pen

So he speaks choreography to the rhythm of opened minds

But he knows self discovery

Like Langston Hughes knows rivers

The lesson flows ever on

An Angel reminded him of his deliverance

That the blessing in his speech started at his feet

See some people find their defining moment

In a number of circumstances

This young man learned to give love

To the beat of the rhythm of night life

She was generous enough to give him that back

And he never found a relationship on that floor

But he had dates with self confidence

Now he has a moment with God

Reminded him of a journey

That ended with the nurturing of a man

Illuminated by the grace of an Angel who remembered

And begun with only a dance

In´no va´tor *n.*: someone who helps to open up a new line of research or technology or art [syn: pioneer, trailblazer, groundbreaker]

- www.dictionary.com

www.ingramcontent.com/pod-product-compliance
Lightning Source LLC
Chambersburg PA
CBHW031526040426
42445CB00009B/408